GOD LISTENS
When You're Sad

GOD LISTENS
When You're Sad

PRAYERS WHEN YOUR ANIMAL FRIEND IS SICK OR DIES

CAROL J. ADAMS

THE PILGRIM PRESS   CLEVELAND

for

BROWNIE, CYRANO, DEMETER,

VEDA, DONNER, SAVANNAH, AND STRIPES,

SITTING IN GOD'S LAP

The Pilgrim Press, 700 Prospect Avenue, Cleveland, Ohio 44115-1100
thepilgrimpress.com
Copyright © 2005 Carol J. Adams

Printed in the United States of America on acid-free paper

10   09   08   07   06   05   5   4   3   2   1

Library of Congress Cataloging-in-Publication Data

Adams, Carol J.
    God listens when you're sad : prayers when your animal friend is sick or dies /
  Carol J. Adams.
      p.   cm.
    ISBN 0-8298-1667-4 (pbk. : alk. paper)
    1. Prayers for animals.   2. Pet owners—Prayer-books and devotions—
English.   3. Children and death.   4. Bereavement in children.   5. Grief in
children.   I. Title.

BV283.A63.A34   2005
242'.8—dc22

                                                          2004063768

Dear Friend,

I'm really sorry you are so sad right now.

I know what it means to love an animal deeply.

I am sure you have had many special times with your animal friend.

You have been given so much! So much joy, so much friendship, so much love.

None of these experiences prepared you for this—this sadness, this worry, this loneliness.

I wrote these prayers because there have been times when I wished for something like this. Something that would help me in my sadness, help me with my worries, help me with my loneliness.

Your sadness tells you something very important—you have loved someone very much.

These prayers tell you something, too: You are not alone in your sadness. Someone listens; Someone cares; Someone is your Friend.

When I have felt so sad I thought no one could understand or help me, I found out that there was Someone Who Listened.

It is very hard to be worried about an animal friend; it is hard when an animal friend is sick and dies. I know

5

because many of my animal friends have died. But praying to God about how you feel and your worries and sadness and grief can be very helpful.

In the prayers that follow, I have left a space for you to name your special animal friend. You can write the name in the space if you would like. Sometimes in a prayer, I use the word "he" and sometimes I use the word "she." You can change these words in any prayer so that it refers accurately to your animal friend. And of course you can skip the prayers that don't apply to your situation.

If there is a prayer you wish I had included, please feel free to let me know. You can write me care of The Pilgrim Press or by email to cja@caroljadams.com.

Even if it feels that very few people understand your special friendship with an animal, don't let that worry you. Not everyone has experienced the joy you have known. I like to think of God as the Friend Who Understands. With this Friend, you can be honest about your feelings; with this Friend, you can share your anger, your grief, your worries. This Friend understands all friendships. This Friend will listen.

Dear God,

Let me tell you about my animal friend.

My animal friend is named _____ .

_____ has lived with my family

  since _____ .

The things I especially have loved about

_____ are:

[*List your favorite things*]

1. _____

2. _____

3. _____

4. _____

5. _____

6. _____

But God, there is something else you need to know:

_____ is sick.

Very, very sick.

What can I do to help, God?

I don't think I can love _____ any

more than I already do.

But I can tell you about my friend.

Can you love _____ as much as I do?

This is what I pray.

Dear God,

_____ is sick.

I can tell.

_____ isn't the same as he has

always been.

My family is trying to take care of _____ .

We are very worried.

We are trying to help _____ feel

better.

Can you help us?

Please help us care for _____ .

Please help _____ feel better.

Dear God,

_____ is very, very sick.

I am scared.

We are taking _____ to the vet.

I know that I see the doctor when I am sick and

animals see a doctor when they are sick.

But it is scary. The vet can't ask _____

what is wrong the way my doctor asks me.

I would like to know what is wrong.

I want _____ to get better.

Please God, send your healing to _____ .

Please God, guide the eyes, ears, and heart of our

vet today.

Dear God,

I pray for the hands of the vet.

May they be steady and quick.

I pray for the heart of the vet.

May it be loving and tender.

I pray for the patients of the vet.

May they be healed.

I pray for the friends of the patients of the vet—

   Like me.

May we be comforted.

May I be comforted.

Please be with me.

Please be with _____ .

Please be with the vet.

Dear God,

It doesn't seem possible that _____

     is getting old.

How can this be happening?

_____ is sleeping so much more.

Seeing _____ getting old scares me.

I know that we are all changing.

I know that every day, each of us changes.

But it is hard to be happy about change when it

     means that _____ is getting old.

Help me to learn how to take care of

_____ now.

Help me to learn to live with the changes

_____ is going through.

Dear God,

I'm not hungry.

I don't want to do anything.

Everyone says I need to eat something.

Everyone says I need to do something.

I am doing something!

I am feeling sad.

And I am doing something more:

I am praying to you.

God, I am not hungry.

God, there is nothing more I want to do.

When will I stop feeling this way?

Please be with me God.

Dear God,

I hate the word "only."

Is that okay?

I am so confused.

People say to me, _____ is only an
  animal.

ONLY?

What gives them the right to say that?

But this is what I am going to do:

when they say, "only,"

I will smile, because I know

my friend _____ is only an animal

in the same way that you are the Only God.

Nothing can compare to you.

And right now, nothing can compare to my
  friendship with _____ .

You understand, don't you?

Dear God,

I feel like screaming.

I feel like stomping up and down stairs.

I feel like throwing my pillow.

I feel like saying "no" all the time.

Why is this happening?

It's not fair.

I am very angry with you, God!

It's okay to be angry with you, isn't it?

I don't scare you, do I?

You've been angry, haven't you?

And you understand me, don't you?

Hear me, God.

Help me, God.

Dear God,

I know _____ is going to die.

_____ won't be here when I come

 home every day.

Who will greet me the way _____

 did?

Who will I take care of?

Who will I feed?

Who will wake me up in the morning?

How will I love anyone as I love _____ ?

God, I feel awful.

Knowing _____ is going to die is a

 terrible thing to know.

Not knowing what I am going to do is terrible, too.

Please share this burden with me;

I don't think I can bear it alone.

Dear God,

This is the hardest thing I have ever had to do.

I do not want to say good-bye.

I do not want _____ to leave us.

I am upset. I don't want this to be happening!

But I know I cannot argue about this. Or . . .

I could argue and yet it will still come to this—

I have to say good-bye.

God, it is time. Somehow, I must understand that it

    is time.

I must release _____ .

_____ is suffering.

I need _____ , but _____

    needs something else.

God, help me with the hardest thing I have ever

    had to do . . .

God, give me the ability to say good-bye.

God, take _____ into your hands.

God, please be with us all today—and greet

_____ for me.

Dear God,

Something very sad has happened.

_____ died.

_____ is gone.

_____ stopped living.

I will never see _____ again.

No more heartbeats.

No more breathing, eating, sleeping.

No more love returned.

It hurts so much.

Help me, God.

God,

My body hurts.

I feel like I want to throw up.

My head feels too heavy.

God, give me a hug.

Dear God,

My friend _____ died.

I am very sad.

I don't understand why _____ died.

Why did _____ have to die?

I wish _____ could come back,

    but I know he won't.

I want _____ to be here with me

    now.

Then I would feel so much better.

He made me so very happy.

But God, please welcome _____

    into heaven for me.

Please take care of _____ for me.

I love him so.

Dear God,

My whole family is so sad.

Please help us to get through this, together.

Help us not to yell at each other because

    we are so sad.

Help us to talk together about _____ .

Thank you for my family.

Stay nearby, today, God, because we all need you.

Dear God,

Can't anyone speak plain English any more?

_____ died.

People say to me _____

    "passed away"

    or "went away"

    or has "gone to sleep."

I didn't "lose" _____ , as though I

    could misplace my friend!

NO!

_____ died.

It is so sad.

I am going to miss _____ so much.

Who can understand this?

I pray that you do.

Dear God,

God, I want you to know that we buried

_____ .

I will always know where her body is.

I can go to that special place and remember her.

Help me not to forget _____ .

Help me to remember.

Help me to remember what she looked like when

the sun was shining on her.

I have put things in a special place to remember her.

I have planted flowers for her.

I don't want to forget _____ .

God, I remember to pray to you,

Help me remember to think of _____ .

God,

Can prayers stay the same?

Can I tell you again and again that

    I am so sad?

Why can't you take away this sadness?

God, I did not know I could cry so much.

Please God, can you help me with my sadness?

Can you wipe my tears?

God, will you listen to this same prayer over

    and over again?

Because I know I'm not done praying it.

Dear God,

I want so much to say:

If only _____ hadn't gotten sick.

If only the vet could have cured _____ .

If only there were no death.

If only I could have saved _____ .

If only you had listened to my prayers and kept

_____ from dying.

There, I said it!

I think I feel a little better.

I know I can't change what happened;

    if only I could!

But I do know that I'm not alone.

I do know that my anger doesn't scare you.

I do know that all beings die.

Thank you for being with me now.

Dear God,

There is so much I don't understand about death;

except I know I will never see

_____ again.

I know death is final.

But I don't understand why it has to be this way.

And just because death is final doesn't mean I have

stopped loving _____ .

I know

with all my body,

with all my heart,

with all my soul

I loved _____ and

_____ loved me.

I do understand this.

Thank you for this love.

God,

Why did _____ have to die?

This just isn't right!

I still needed her, and she needed me.

It isn't fair.

Someone said, "Life isn't fair."

Well, why isn't it?

Someone said, "God needed _____."

I don't believe it.

You don't work that way, do you, God?

You know I needed her more.

Who will take care of me now?

Who will take care of her?

Will she be cold?

Will she sit in the sunshine?

Are you taking care of her?

I wish I could know for sure.

Dear God,

Sometimes when I feel happy I feel like I am

betraying _____ .

I feel I am betraying _____ because

I'm not feeling sad all the time.

It's okay to feel happy and sad, isn't it?

I know I'm not done feeling sad.

I'm sad to be without _____ .

But I'm happy, too.

I am happy to have the memories of

_____ .

I am happy looking at pictures of _____ .

I can be both happy and sad, can't I?

I'm learning different ways of remembering, aren't I?

Thank you for this.

Dear God,

Is _____ happy there with you?

Do you know the special things _____

loves?

Because I did.

Does he get to play with you?

Do you know his nickname?

Do you know his favorite food?

I wish I could see _____ there with

you.

God, are you watching over _____ ?

I wish that one more time I could watch over

_____ , too.

Are you watching over me, God?

Because I need you, God.

Dear God,

So much has changed because _____

    died.

Death changes everything.

I've changed, too.

How will my friends view me now?

Can they tell I've changed?

Will they treat me differently?

Even if I can't stay the same,

I want some things to stay the same, like my

    friendships.

Walk with me today, God,

Walk with my friends and me.

Dear God,

You know that _____ is dead.

I have prayed to you before about how sad I am.

But now I understand something.

My sadness shows me something about myself.

I loved deeply.

I loved _____ so much.

Even though I am sad, I am learning to understand
    this sadness.

My sadness is a sign that I loved.

Thank you for _____ .

Thank you for teaching me about love.

But please be with me because I am still so sad.

Dear God,

I feel so lonely without _____ .

If _____ were here,

    she would understand

    how lonely I feel.

Always, she was here.

Always, I wasn't alone . . .

    until now.

I need you. I feel so alone.

Please hear my prayer.

    Please hear my prayer so that I know

    I am not alone.

Dear God,

Today, I just want to remember _____ .

> I remember the way she moved.
>
> I remember the way she smelled.
>
> I remember the special things we would do
>
>   together—she and I.
>
> I remember when she arrived—how exciting
>
>   that was!
>
> I remember her in the morning time.
>
> I remember her at nighttime.
>
> And I remember how she died.

Dear God, it is good to remember.

_____ was so special!

This is what I will always have, isn't it?

I will always have these special memories.

Thank you, God.

Dear God,

Please stay near me today.

Last night I dreamt that _____ was

   alive.

It was so wonderful to play with him again.

It seemed just right.

But now I am awake and I know it was just a

   dream.

I wish I could have stayed in my dream.

I woke up and I was so sad.

Was _____ coming to say good-bye?

Was _____ telling me that he's

   okay now?

Did you give me this dream as a gift?

Thank you for _____ .

And thank you for my dream.

Dear God,

There is something I need to say.

I have been thinking about these words!

I wish I had said them to _____ .

Now I realize I can tell you.

I have a sense that by telling you, _____

   will hear it too.

Here is what I wish I had said:

_____

_____

_____

_____

Thank you, God, for listening.

Thank you, God, for hearing these special words.

Dear God,

I still miss _____ .

Someone said to me, "You will get over it."

Why would I want to "get over it"?

I loved _____ and I miss her.

If I hadn't loved _____ , I wouldn't

miss her.

But since I loved _____ , I *do* miss

her.

The *missing* is part of the loving.

And I don't want to get over it.

I know _____ is dead.

I still don't understand why.

Maybe that is what I will get over—

not understanding.

Can you teach me to understand?

And until then, can you comfort me?

Because I still miss _____ .

Dear God,

It is getting hard to remember _____ .

God, help me remember.

God, I have a special memory I never want to forget.

This special memory is:

_____

_____

_____

_____

_____

_____

_____

_____

God, share this memory with me.

Help me remember.

Dear God,

I've been thinking of all the sadness you must
learn about.

I know how sad I feel.

You know, too, because I have told you.

And I have friends who have been so sad, too.

And yet God, you aren't alone, are you?

I know _____ is with you.

Right now, you must be amidst dogs who are
sticking their noses all over the place and dogs
who are wagging their tails!

And you must be with cats who are purring and
cats who are stretching!

Salamanders must be turning beautiful colors
nearby you.

You are among guinea pigs, and rabbits, snakes, turtles, and birds, aren't you?

The fishes themselves must be breathtaking!

God, are you playing with them right now?

Even with all the animals there, every one is special to you, right, God?

Is _____ in your lap right now?

Is that why you can hear about so much sadness?

You are never alone, are you?

In the space on this page, you can write your own prayer. Tell God what you want to say about your animal friend or about your feelings.

_____

_____

_____

_____

_____

_____

_____

_____

_____

_____

In the space on this page, you can draw a picture or paste a photograph of your special friend.

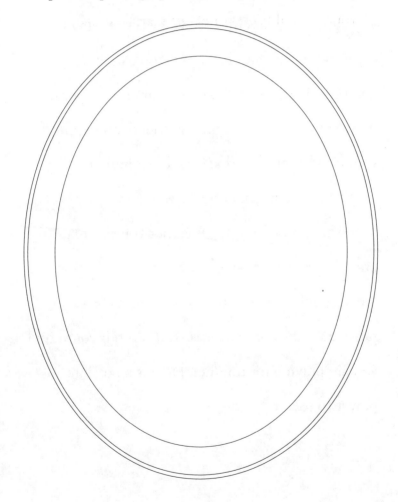

A note to family

Your child's love for animals is a gift from God. You can help your child grieve by simply staying close to him/her and listening. You can answer questions honestly, talk about your child's special friendship with his/her animal friend, and remind your child every day that you love him/her.

You can help your child create a memory box of his/her animal friend. Together you can read prayers aloud. Or you can say to your child that you are available if any of the prayers he/she is saying raises questions or concerns. You can tell your child you are praying for him/her. Here is a possible prayer to use:

A PRAYER FOR CHILDREN

Dear God,

We are all so sad.

But, God, I pray now for my child _____.

Please be present to _____ as she/he

   prays to you.

Please help her/him know comfort in the midst

   of grief;

Your presence in the face of loneliness.

Please help us provide a healing presence

   to each other.

Please, God, help us fill the empty space

   in our house

with love and understanding,

with listening and support.

Remind each of us, God, that we are not alone.

45

THANKS

Some people and animals helped me write this book. Thank you to my sons Douglas and Benjamin for loving Holly, Silver, Domino, Snowball, and Leia with me and my spouse. And thank you to Brownie, Cyrano, Demeter, Veda, Donner, Savannah, Stripes, and many others who taught me about friendships with animals.

RELATED TITLES FROM THE PILGRIM PRESS

WATER BUGS & DRAGONFLIES
Explaining Death to Young Children (revised)
Doris Stickney
ISBN 0-8298-1624-0/paper/23 pages/$3.00

LEAVING HOME WITH FAITH
Nurturing the Spiritual Life of Our Youth
Elizabeth F. Caldwell
ISBN 0-8298-1504-X/paper/144 pages/$16.00

MAKING A HOME FOR FAITH
Nurturing the Spiritual Life of Your Children
Elizabeth F. Caldwell
ISBN 0-8298-1370-5/paper/118 pages/$15.00

ANIMAL RITES
Liturgies of Animal Care
Andrew Linzey
ISBN 0-8298-1451-5/paper/186 pages/$16.00

THE STORY OF JESUS
Mark Water and Susie Poole
ISBN 0-8298-1460-4/paper over board/32 pages/$12.00

THE PILGRIM BOOK OF BIBLE STORIES
ISBN 0-8298-1487-6/paper over board/320 pages/$22.50

DANIEL AND THE LION
Sekiya Miyoshi
ISBN 0-8298-1452-3/paper over board/28 pages/$14.00

DAVID AND GOLIATH
Sekiya Miyoshi
ISBN 0-8298-1453-1/paper over board/28 pages/$14.00

JACOB'S LADDER
Sekiya Miyoshi
ISBN 0-8298-1454-X/paper over board/28 pages/$14.00

JONAH AND THE BIG FISH
Sekiya Miyoshi
ISBN 0-8298-1511-2/paper over board/28 pages/$14.00

To order these or any other books from The Pilgrim Press, call or write to:

THE PILGRIM PRESS
700 PROSPECT AVENUE
CLEVELAND, OH 44115-1100

Phone orders: 800·537·3394 (M–F, 8:30AM–4:30PM ET)
Fax orders: 216·736·2206

Please include shipping charges of $5.00 for the first book and 75¢ for each additional book.

Or order from our Web site at thepilgrimpress.com.

Prices subject to change without notice.